D1237627

Gloria Swanson

Gloria Swanson

Richard M. Hudson and Raymond Lee

South Brunswick and New York: A. S. Barnes and Company

London: Thomas Yoseloff Ltd

A. S. Barnes and Co., Inc.
Cranbury, New Jersey 08512

Thomas Yoseloff Ltd
108 New Bond Street
London W1Y OQX, England

SBN 498 07494 3

Printed in the United States of America

Contents

Gloria Swanson

1

Image and Woman

Hollywood Boulevard has been famous around the world for its promenade of stars, whether it was Valentino dashing to work in his Isotta Fraschini, Charlie Chaplin and Paulette Goddard window-shopping, or for its greatest moment in 1925 when Gloria Swanson returned from picture making in Europe, and was greeted by more than 100,000 fans who spilled their welcome like champagne.

Twenty-five years later, following a reign of unmatched popularity, still glamorous but now a has-been, her star was reborn on another Boulevard, Sunset.

As a slightly mad silent movie queen she gave a performance that almost won her a sound Oscar in Billy Wilder's *Sunset Boulevard.*

How did this super star reach her orbit in the Hollywood heavens?

Much has been said and written but La Swanson's own words seem the best down through the years:

"I was never 'screen-struck.' I did not think of the movies as a road to fame and fortune. And I spent no weary weeks at the studio gates waiting for my chance.

"An impulse, or perhaps it may better be called a hunch, was responsible for my introduction into motion pictures.

"My only interest in acting had been confined to school plays. The first appearance I ever made was as a child of seven, when I had a singing role in a benefit performance at Key West, Florida, where my father, an army officer, was stationed at the time. I do not remember whether the benefit was a brilliant success. Certainly my part in it could not have been exceptional.

"On another occasion, in Puerto Rico, I was the leading lady of an operetta given by my school. I have been told since that time that my

9

natural talent was the subject of numerous comments, but I paid little attention to the remarks of elders. I only knew that I enjoyed doing such things.

"Later in 1914, I returned to Chicago to finish my schooling in the city of my birth. One day my aunt suggested a visit to the Essanay Studios. Up to this time I had taken no particular interest in motion pictures, but I welcomed the opportunity to visit the studio in order to satisfy my natural curiosity. I was then fifteen years old.

"Once past the gate of the studio I was fascinated. It was all so new to me, so different. And then came the hunch. Almost without realizing what I was saying, I expressed a desire to appear before the cameras. A director who stood nearby heard my remark and in a few days I was given the opportunity to fulfill it. I was called for work at a studio!

"My first appearance was not as an extra, but as a bit player. I was thrilled. In the second picture, however, I appeared only as an extra, sitting at a cafe table. After that I was given further bits.

"As time went on, I became more and more fascinated and made the most of every opportunity to learn all there was to learn. In three months I was made a stock player, which meant I was guaranteed four days' pay each week, at $3.25 a day, whether I worked or not.

"I was cast for a bit in Charlie Chaplin's first Essanay picture, *His New Job.* Chaplin was supposed to kick me in the caboose. But after a dozen rehearsals he fired me. He was quite right. I was terrible.

"On leaving Essanay, I decided to journey to California. After two weeks in Los Angeles I went to Mack Sennett at the Keystone studio and was signed to a picture following a brief rehearsal. Then I made one picture at Universal.

"Returning to Keystone Mack Sennett offered me a contract. I held out for $75.00 a week with an increase of ten dollars every three months or so and I got it.

"I appeared in a number of Sennett comedies costarred with Bobby Vernon. But during my work there, for a year and a half I never was cast as a 'bathing beauty.' The general belief that I was once a Sennett bathing girl is erroneous."

Swanson seems to have a "thing" going about this last statement despite the fact many top stars started as bathing girls.

Clarence Badger, then a Keystone writer and trying for his first directorial assignment, recalled his first meeting with Swanson and Wallace Beery, then her husband, and pertinent facts about their association:*

"The girl I judged to be about eighteen. I was surprised, pleasantly

---

* Permission to reprint granted by Clarence Badger. This quotation originally appeared in *Image,* No. 51, May, 1957.

so. She was charming. Her figure was petite and shapely. Her face and eyes were unusually beautiful, a kind of winsome, appealing beauty. She radiated personality.

"I asked her to remove her hat, a narrow-brimmed, flower-decorated straw of the style of those days. She stood there fingering it nervously as I studied her.

" 'I don't believe I'd heard your name,' I said.

" 'Gloria Swanson,' she informed me.

" 'Well, don't be nervous, Miss Swanson,' I said, 'be yourself—might as well now as any time. We are going to see a lot of each other during the next few weeks, you know. Come on now—relax.'

" 'Yes—of course,' she said, smiling.

"Yes, she had definite possibilities for my heroine. However, the important thing was, could she act?

"I asked Beery if he had any acting experience.

" 'I did a series of Comedies for Essanay impersonating a Swedish maid. That's where I met Gloria. The two of us thought we'd crash Hollywood, and, well, see if we could make the grade.'

" 'I'm pleased to hear that,' I said. 'And I'll prophesy here and now that if you both play ball with me you'll have crashed Hollywood when the picture's finished. We haven't a story yet so the first thing we'll do is dope one out."

"Just then Bobby Vernon popped his head in the door.

"So arm in arm on a fine sunny day I took Gloria, Wally and Bobby for a walk.

"We climbed to the top of a grass-clad hill which overlooked the Keystone studios. There I divulged my pent-up plans. I had a lot of things to prove to Mr. Sennett. I assured them that if by our joint efforts a knockout job did result, not only myself, but all, would be well set in pictures.

"Enthusiasm grew. Bobby had a wonderful inborn sense of comedy. Gloria was radiant. She sparkled with ideas. Wally the same. A fresh and interesting story started growing.

"Following the finish of our picture I went back to writing gags. When Mr. Sennett returned from New York I waited nervously. Later he rushed into my office shouting: 'It's a bear, Badger, a bear.' Which sounded like a pun, badger-bear. As he continued: 'That Swanson dame's sure got it—swell. That Beery bird, too—great. And Vernon—what a revelation! We'll team the three of them—sure-fire box office.'

"And so began the series of Keystone comedies I made with Gloria Swanson which included: *Haystacks and Steeples, The Nick of Time Baby, Teddy at the Throttle, The Pullman Bride, Whose Baby.*

"Gloria Swanson was wonderful to work with. Even then, in those youthful days, she was most talented, appealing and charming; definitely possessing screen personality to such an outstanding degree, that it was easy to forsee she would go a long way in pictures."

Mabel Normand was the silents' queen of comedy. No one in silent films ever matched her delightful antics that had fans calling her a female Chaplin.

One day the King of Comedy quipped to Swanson that he was going to make her a second Mabel. She snapped back that she'd never be a second anybody and walked off the lot.

Fortunately for her, Triangle Pictures had been watching her and she walked into their spotlight to star in eight domestic dramas. The year was 1918. A few miles away at Paramount Cecil B. DeMille waited like Moses to bring Gloria into the promised land.

DeMille remembered Swanson:*

"I first saw authority as well as beauty in Gloria Swanson's simple leaning against a door in a Mack Sennett comedy. I saw the future that she could have in pictures if her career was properly handled.

"Many actors who can be magnificently hateful villains always want to play Little Bo-Peep. But Gloria Swanson suffered from no such illusions. I never told her, until after her first few successes under my direction, why I was handling her career in a certain way, but she was intelligent enough to know and patient enough to wait.

"Nothing was spared to bring out all the glamour that was Gloria. But I did not star her. She received the same billing as any other member of the cast; she also received, was contented with, a relatively small salary. The public, not I, made Gloria Swanson a star.

"When the time came, I said to her: Now, young fellow, go and be a star. You don't need me anymore. But Gloria chose to remain under my direction for six pictures in all, before going on to become the reigning queen of the movies."

During this period Swanson, who had separated from Beery a month after their marriage in 1916, finally divorced the character actor who was later to reach his peak at MGM.

The first of five husbands had gone and with not even a footnote. It was an odd marriage for both, but their brief relationship had brought them to the cinema wonderland where they found a brimming pot of gold and world acclaim.

In 1919 she married Herbert K. Somborn, owner of the famous Brown Derby Restaurant by whom she had her first child, Gloria. Later when this union broke up she commented cryptically:

---

* From Cecil B. DeMille's Autobiography published by Prentice-Hall, Inc., Englewood Cliffs, N.J. Used by permission.

"I not only believe in divorce, I sometimes think I don't believe in marriage at all."

At this time she was playing in De Millers with such titles as: *Don't Change Your Husband, Why Change Your Wife?* and *For Better, For Worse.*

It was during this period that critics tagged Swanson a "clothes horse." Everything she would do in one of the DeMille dramas was copied—hair, hats, shoes, gowns of all description. And when the immortal director dunked her in the famous *Male and Female* bathtub scene, the plumbers of the land cheered her. Never had there been such a run on sunken and marbled indoor immersers.

When Paramount elevated her to stardom—whether by *her* design or the exigencies of a maturing industry—she began to show signs of being an actress with a variety of roles that ranged from a gum-chewing clerk, a Parisian gamine-Apache to a Balkan queen.

A star was born. And a mother. In 1923, she adopted a four-month-old boy, whom she named Joseph Swanson.

This segment of Gloria's career was climaxed in 1924 by the filming of the pretentious *Madame Sans-Gene,* in France. This is the story of the laundress who befriended Napoleon and later became the wife of a Marshal. Here she met her third husband and thereafter signed her name with a royal hand—*Marquise de la Falaise de la Coudraye.*

Adolph Zukor, Paramount head, following her tremendous triumphant return to Hollywood and subsequent overwhelming success on even mediocre films, offered her a new contract at $18,000 a week. Gloria refused, so he upped the ante to a million a year. Only Mary Pickford had ever received such a sum. But Gloria turned it down.

Of this break with the studio that had made her the queen of the screen, she said in 1930:

"In 1926, I became an owner-member of United Artists, and an independent producer. I am finding greater happiness in my work than ever before. And I hope the public which has been so good to me, will find this new enthusiasm in my pictures."

Joseph P. Kennedy supplied the money and under this aegis Swanson gave what most critics agreed was her finest silent performance as the South Seas shady-lady, Sadie Thompson. She also proved she could do battle with any of the Hollywood powers and win. When Will Hays, President of the Motion Picture Producers and Distributors and the man who wielded the censor's scissors on all material, refused to give her permission to film the sensational Somerset Maugham

13

story and play, *Rain*, she changed the title to *Sadie Thompson*. The minister, who fell prey to Sadie's charms while trying to save her soul, gave way to a morals reformer without clerical garb. The result was shattering in many areas.

With a taboo film a hit at the box-office and power burning her fingertips she chose Erich von Stroheim, Hollywood's most famous writer-director of erotica, to bring in her next production.

Frustrated by Stroheim's demand for details that delayed filming and shot costs sky-high, *Queen Kelly,* the tale of a convent girl's gambols with a prince and a mad queen and her rise as owner of a string of African brothels, was cancelled out a third way through at a loss of $800,000.

Years later she renewed production and this version was released in Europe and South America with a modicum of success.

Following the dissolution of her partnership with Kennedy, she dissolved her marriage to the Marquis who summed it up with: "I married a business woman." Later the Marquis married Constance Bennett who was a pretty fair business woman herself. She became the first star to get $30,000 a week from Warner Bros.

Swanson's fourth plunge into the marital cataracts featured handsome Irish sportsman Michael Farmer. She tried and failed to make him an actor. But another daughter, Michelle Bridget, was a happy highlight of this marriage-go-round, which ran for three years.

The ensuing years showed a decline in her career after she finished her United Artists sojourn. At MGM Irving Thalberg signed her for a remake of Elinor Glyn's sex-sational novel, *Three Weeks,* but his untimely death ended this. At Fox she costarred with John Boles in a so-so production of the Kern-Hammerstein hit, *Music in the Air.*

Following the mediocre *Music in the Air,* Gloria became a gadabout, touring the world and indulging for the first time her second passion—being a businesswoman. Under such names as *Puritan Dress Company* and *Essence of Nature Cosmetics,* she hit the fashion, cosmetic and health foods markets with as much drama as on the day she took her famous bath in DeMille's *Male and Female.*

"My feeling is that beauty is strictly internal. It comes from within, and concerns one's circulation, and I don't mean the newspaper kind."

Food plays a leading role in Swanson's beauty routine.

"People eat too much and too rich foods. My pepper-upper is sea moss for breakfast. I just start the day on a wave of energy. All my vegetables are organically grown. Sometimes I'll nibble liver or a little fish."

On cosmetics:

"The best cosmetics are in our own ice box—cucumbers, fruit, eggs. Papaya is good for bruises. Your grandmother used corn meal on her face. It's just old-fashioned good sense. Witch doctor stuff.

"I'm a witch doctor, and a food faddist. I grind my own rock salt, I get special olive oil, special honey which I use instead of sugar."

As Angela Taylor reported:

When Miss Swanson travels to promote her dress line for Puritan— "Death of a Saleswoman, I call it"—she carries along her own food and adds, "I put half of it on my face."

"I've never had a dull moment in my life. I've always wanted to try something new. I had the first pantie girdle, the first broad-tail suit, the first sack dress—from Givenchy."

Is there a formula for being attractive?

"Yes, stop acquiring so many eye-catching focal points. Special hats, bags, gloves, collars. Instead make the most of your own best facial features. Mouth, teeth, eyes or hair. Whatever it is, accentuate it."

In 1941 the lure of films drew her again before the camera in *Father Takes a Wife,* with Adolph Menjou at RKO. A fifth marriage was added with William H. Davey. It was a short run—of 44 days and then divorce.

Turning to the legitimate theatre she took to the boards with the same gusto she had shown before the cameras. Notable among several plays was *Twentieth Century,* a spoof on a stage producer and his star-lover in which she costarred with Jose Ferrer on Broadway in 1950.

In this same year she made the most famous screen comeback of all movie history, that of Norma Desmond in Billy Wilder's *Sunset Boulevard.* The picture also reunited Swanson with Paramount Studios for the first time in 24 years. "I just want to tell you how happy I am to be back in the studio making a picture again"—a direct quote from the film that won Academy Awards for best screenplay, music, and art direction.

Sunset Boulevard was the most "inside," sharp and accurate portrait of cinemaland ever put on celluloid. It was a bare-bones portrait of a woman who could be, but was not, Swanson. But there was enough Desmond in Swanson to make everyone believe both were one and the same.

The new Hollywood has little respect for the old, and even less for a film that reminds it of the golden greatness of the past. For this reason, you are only as good as your last film. Another irony: Gloria Swanson received second billing to William Holden except in the European release prints.

The picture was filmed on the Paramount lot and in a fabulous mansion built in the roaring twenties, which seemed almost human in the way it dominated the characters.

A highlight scene: Norma is screening some films in which she starred for her lover Joe. One fantastic scene is a candlelighted head-shot of Swanson. It has been called the $800,000 closeup. In 1928 it had been shot for Swanson's illfated *Queen Kelly*.

This Academy Award Nominee Film also contained a memorable impersonation of Charlie Chaplin by Swanson. She had also done this in *Manhandled* made in 1924.

At the Hollywood Wax Museum in Buena Park, California, the three key figures—Swanson, William Holden and Eric von Stroheim—are captured for all time. The star donated a $10,000 chinchilla cape for the wax figure and a fresh carnation is placed in her outstretched hand daily.

All Hollywood was disappointed when Swanson lost the Oscar to Judy Holliday. The struggle for the award was between Swanson's fabulous performance and that of Bette Davis in *All About Eve*. The tension was so strong, the consensus agreed, that the Academy of Motion Picture Arts and Sciences could not choose between them and gave the Oscar to Miss Holliday merely for repeating her stage role in *Born Yesterday*.

The Academy evening was also Swanson's birthday. The ladies in competition waited along with Jose Ferrer at New York's Zambra cafe.

When the final envelope was opened and the name read, Swanson, tears in eyes, congratulated Holliday and then said, "My dear, couldn't you have waited? You have so much ahead of you, so many years, and this was my only chance."

It was also Judy Holliday's; later, she lost her life to cancer.

On May 8, 1967, the New York Theatre Organ Society, Inc., paid her special tribute by presenting a program of Gloria Swanson from silents to sound, at the Beacon Theatre.

The program read:

"Long before Hollywood made stars, there were stars who made Hollywood." Gloria Swanson was one of them. She was the first American to receive the George Eastman House Award for "outstanding contributions to the art of cinema"—an honor granted previously only to Garbo and Chaplin.

And as a chafing footnote, though she appeared in several minor films after *Sunset Boulevard*, it *was* her only chance for an Oscar. Paramount didn't even look for a follow-up property to their hit and the greatest comeback in movies.

But as she has repeatedly said: "This old war-horse has got to keep searching. There must be another great role in some script writer's head somewhere in Hollywood . . . for me . . ."

2

Her Fabulous Face

HER EARLY CAREER

The following portraits were taken during the late teens and early 20s when Miss Swanson's career was just beginning.

Personally autographed for the author, Mr. Hudson.

23

49

Gloria
Swanson
by ALFRED CHENEY JOHNSTON

This is probably the most famous portrait ever taken of Gloria Swanson. It would hardly create a stir today, but in 1924, when Edward Steichen made it for the magazine Vanity Fair, *it was something of a sensation. Photographers were sure it was a double exposure. Shooting through a veil was, apparently, another Steichen innovation.*

Gloria Swanson

(Courtesy Paramount Pictures)

THE LATE 20s AND THE EARLY 30s

During this period Miss Swanson made a successful transition from silent to sound films.

(Courtesy Russell Ball)

(Courtesy Clarence Sinclair Bull)

(Courtesy Fox Film, photo by Otto Dyar)

(Courtesy Fox Film, photo by Otto Dyar)

(Courtesy Fox Film, photo by Otto Dyar)

(Courtesy Russell Ball)

"*Mona Lisa Swanson.*" *John Decker, the distinguished artist and caricaturist, offers his impression of Gloria as the famous lady of Da Vinci's painting and mischievous sketch of her as the arch prima donna of* Tonight or Never.

69

THE LATE 30s AND 40s

The ensuing years saw a decline in her career which eventually turned her to the stage.

Four photos of Miss Swanson by Clarence Sinclair Bull.

Personally autographed for the author, Mr. Hudson.

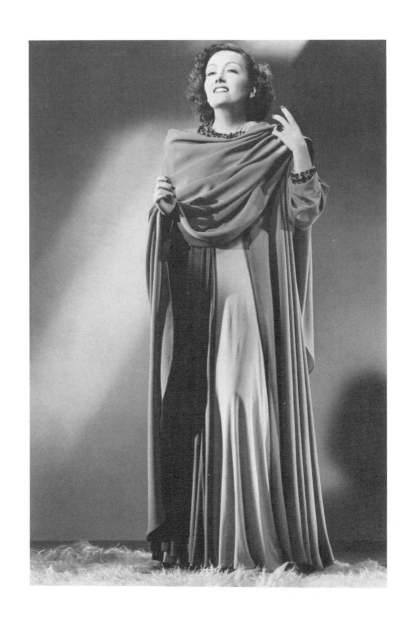

Time has not diminished the beauty of the "Glamor Queen."

This portrait was used for Miss Swanson's beauty ads in the early 1950s.

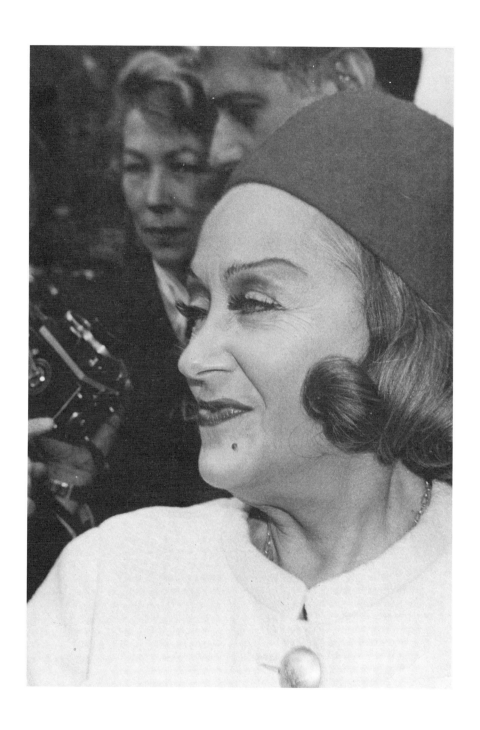

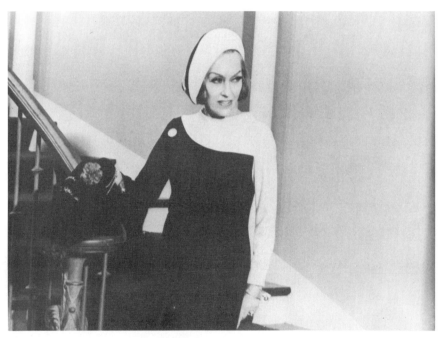

Portrait taken in 1966 on the set of "The Beverly Hillbillies."

3
Behind the Scenes

In the early teens with her first husband, Wallace Beery.

A rare portrait with her father, Joseph T. Swanson (during the late teens or early 20s).

Gloria with (from top left) director Sam Wood, Elinor Glyn, who wrote several Swanson films, and Theodore Kosloff.

Mack Sennett, the King of Comedy, has just reminded her of the good old days when she earned $65 a week.

With her husband, the Marquis de la Falaise (during the late 1920s).

With Carole Lombard on the set of We're Not Dressing, *1934.*

Three Hollywood socialites at a Marion Davies party. Gloria on left, Charlie Chaplin center, and Miss Davies on right, 1930.

Old Friends. When Herbert Marshall brought Miss Swanson down to Paramount Studio for a visit, one of the first persons she wanted to see was W. C. Fields.

With Shirley MacLaine and Jack Lemmon on the set of The Apartment, *1960. (Courtesy United Artists Corporation.)*

The four generations of Swansons (left to right): granddaughter, Brooke Anderson; mother, Mrs. Charles Woodruff; daughter, Mrs. Robert W. Anderson; and Gloria.

Oscar Time. Judy Holliday, José Ferrer, and Gloria Swanson sit, drained of emotion, in New York, after the Hollywood presentation of the 1950s Academy Awards. Ferrer won the Oscar for best male performance in Cyrano *and Judy won the female performance award for* Born Yesterday, *winning over Swanson's* Sunset Boulevard.

The beautiful world of Essence Of Nature . . . first original, complete collection in the natural field endowed with a total concept of purity, luxury and effectiveness — at sensible prices.

essence of nature *Cosmetics* . . . secrets of everlasting natural beauty, created by one of the worlds most youthful women — GLORIA SWANSON.

GLORIA SWANSON Ltd. • SYRACUSE, NEW YORK 13201

An ad for her cosmetic firm.

4

Her Films

* This index also appeared in *Films In Review*, April, 1965.

Classic's Family Album

Gloria poses in early Sennett film.

Bathing beauty, 1915 style.

Wallace Beery, Gloria's first husband, starred with her in early Sennett films.

Gloria in 1917 comedy.

With Mack Swain in early Sennett comedy.

Aground in Sennett film.

With Richard Travers and Ruth Stonehouse in The Romance of An American Duchess.

6. 1916: HEARTS & SPARKS. Sennett-Keystone.
   CAST: Hank Mann, Bobby Vernon, Tom Kennedy, Nick Cogley, Billie Bennett, Joe Lee, Charles Parrott.
7. 1916: A SOCIAL CUB. Sennett-Keystone. Directed by Clarence Badger later famed for light comedy.
   CAST: Bobby Vernon, Harry Gribbon, Reggie Morris, Joseph Swickard, Elizabeth DeWitt.
8. 1916: THE DANGER GIRL. Sennett-Keystone.
   CAST: Bobby Vernon.
9. 1916: LOVE ON SKATES. Sennett-Keystone.
   CAST: Bobby Vernon, Myrtle Lind, Helen Bray.
10. 1916: HAYSTACKS & STEEPLES. Sennett-Keystone. Directed by Clarence Badger.
    CAST: Reggie Morris, Bobby Vernon
11. 1916: THE NICK OF TIME BABY. Sennett-Keystone. Directed by Clarence Badger.
    CAST: Bobby Vernon, Sylvia Ashton, Helen Bray, Earl Rodney.
12. 1916: TEDDY AT THE THROTTLE. Sennett-Keystone. Diricted by Clarence Badger this starred the fabulous dog, Teddy.
    CAST: Wallace Beery, Bobby Vernon.
13. 1917: BASEBALL MADNESS. Universal-Victor. Directed by Billy Mason.
    CAST: Billy Mason, Orin Jackson, Countess Du Cello, Marc Fenton.

With Bobby Vernon and Reggie Morris in A Social Cub.

Bobby Vernon is not daunted by kitchen catastrophe in Haystacks and Steeples.

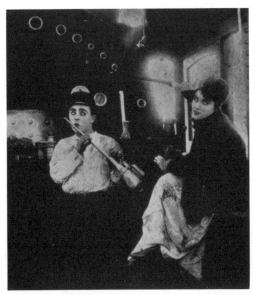

With Bobby Vernon in Teddy at the Throttle.

Top: *with Bobby Vernon in early comedy.* Bottom: *With Mack Swain and Chester Conklin in* Teddy at the Throttle.

14. 1917: DANGERS OF A BRIDE. Sennett-Keystone.
    CAST: Bobby Vernon.
15. 1917: THE SULTAN'S WIFE. Sennett-Keystone.
    CAST: Bobby Vernon, Teddy, the dog, Joseph Callahan.
16. 1917: A PULLMAN BRIDE. Sennett-Keystone. Directed by Clarence Badger.
    CAST: Chester Conklin, Mack Swain.
17. 1918: SOCIETY FOR SALE. Triangle. Directed by Frank Borzage.
    A London mannequin pays an impoverished nobleman to pass her off as his fiancee so she can get into high society. He falls in love with her, and then finds she is herself of the nobility, trying to vindicate her father, who had fallen from grace.
    CAST: William Desmond, Herbert Prior, Charles Dorian, Lillian West, Lillian Langdon.

With William Desmond in Society for Sale.

18. 1918: HER DECISION. Triangle. Directed by Jack Conway.
    A private secretary marries her boss in order to gain money for a sister who has been betrayed—and learns to love the man she married.
    CAST: J. Barney Sherry, Darrell Foss, Ann Kroman.

116

19. 1918: YOU CAN'T BELIEVE EVERYTHING. Triangle. Directed by Jack Conway. Scandal shadows a flirtatious girl's life, but when she rescues a man from drowning, and falls truly in love with him, she doesn't care what the world says.

    CAST: Jack Richardson, Darrell Foss, Edward Piel, Claire McDowell.

Gloria in You Can't Believe Everything, *her first dramatic role.*

With Jack Richardson in You Can't Believe Everything.

20. 1918: EVERYWOMAN'S HUSBAND. Triangle. Directed by Gilbert P. Hamilton. A young wife follows the advice of her domineering mother and nearly drives her husband away. When her father commits suicide she realizes mother didn't know best and becomes a loving wife and regains her husband's devotion.

    CAST: Joe King, Lillian Langdon, George Pearce, Lillian West, Jack Livingston.

21. 1918: SHIFTING SANDS. Triangle. Directed by Albert Parker. A young woman is trapped by a German and railroaded to prison. After her release she marries a wealthy man, and when war breaks out, the German tries to blackmail her into being a secret agent for Germany. But she turns the tables on him.

    CAST: Joe King, Harvey Clark, Leothe Carton, Lillian Langdon, Arthur Millett.

22. 1918: STATION CONTENT. Triangle. Directed by Arthur Hoyt.

    A railroad drama about a wife who, after her baby's death, runs away from the lonely signal station managed by her husband, and goes on the stage. Later, at the risk of her life, she saves a train headed for disaster—and is reunited with her husband.

    CAST: Lee Hill, Arthur Millett, Nellie Allen, Ward Caulfield.

23. 1918: SECRET CODE. Triangle. Directed by Albert Parker. A senator marries a young girl and is stunned when she is suspected of being a spy. However, the "Secret code" being sent through knitted sweaters only contains instructions for knitting a baby's jacket and the real spy, trapped, is forced to confess.

CAST: J. Barney Sherry, Rhy Alexander, Leslie Stewart, Joe King, Dorothy Wallace.

24. 1918: WIFE OR COUNTRY. Triangle. Directed by E. Mason Hopper.

A young woman reforms a brilliant attorney from alcoholism and out of gratitude he marries her. When war comes the wife is trapped into being a spy for Germany, and the husband falls silently in love with his secretary. He learns of his wife's perfidy, and she solves his dilemma by taking poison.

CAST: Harry Mestayer, Jack Richardson, Gretchen Lederer, Charles West.

With Julia Faye and Lew Cody in Don't Change Your Husband.

25. 1919: DON'T CHANGE YOUR HUSBAND. Paramount-Artcraft. Directed by Cecil B. DeMille from screenplay by Jeanie Macpherson. A wife loves her husband, but he, absorbed by business, neglects her. She is attracted to a charming man and her husband gives her a divorce when she requests it. Her new husband neglects her, gambles, drinks, and chases after other women. So she divorces him and re-wins her first husband.

CAST: Elliott Dexter, Lew Cody, Julia Faye, Sylvia Ashton, Theodore Roberts, James Neill.

In Don't Change Your Husband.

26. 1919: FOR BETTER, FOR WORSE. Paramount-Artcraft. An Edgar Selwyn story adapted by Jeanie Macpherson. Directed by Cecil B. DeMille.

A rich young girl denounces her lover, an eminent pediatrician, as a coward when he elects to stay at home and care for crippled children instead of enlisting for World War I. She marries a young man who is off to the battlefields, where he is badly wounded and disfigured. He gets false word home that he has been killed. The girl finds the real worth of the doctor she had denounced and is about to marry him when her husband returns from the dead.

CAST: Elliott Dexter, Tom Forman, Sylvia Ashton, Raymond Hatton, Theodore Roberts, Wanda Hawley, Winter Hall, Jack Holt, Fred Huntley.

In For Better, For Worse.

With Sylvia Ashton in For Better, For Worse.

27. 1919: MALE AND FEMALE. Paramount. Adapted from Sir James A. Barrie's play *The Admirable Crichton.* Directed by Cecil B. DeMille.

Lady Mary and her family are spoiled snobs of England's idle rich. On a cruise, their yacht is wrecked, and they find themselves inhabitants of a tropical island. Their butler and maid-of-all-work now become the rulers and Lady Mary falls in love with her butler. Then everybody is rescued, and back in England, each reverts to his original class of society.

CAST: Thomas Meighan, Lila Lee, Theodore Roberts, Bebe Daniels, Julia Faye, Raymond Hatton, Robert Cain, Edward Burns, Wesley Barry, Mildred Reardon, Maym Kelso, Edna Mae Cooper, Lillian Leighton.

With (left to right) Lila Lee, Mildred Reardon, and Thomas Meighan in Male and Female.

A scene from Male and Female.

With Thomas Meighan and Lila Lee. (Male and Female.)

DeMille's famous bathtub scene in Male and Female.

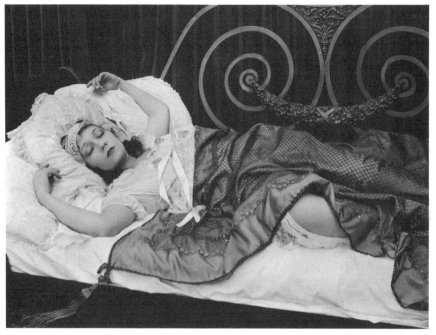

Gloria rests for awhile in Male and Female.

28. 1920: WHY CHANGE YOUR WIFE? Paramount. A Wm. C.
De Mille story with scenario by Olga Printzlau & Sada
Cowan. Directed by Cecil B. DeMille.

A husband sated with a highbrow wife not always care-
ful about her most glamorous appearance becomes fascinated by a pretty little schemer. There is a divorce and a
new marriage, but the first wife, now a glamor girl, sets
out to win him back—and does.

CAST: Thomas Meighan, Bebe Daniels, Theodore Kosloff, Sylvia Ashton, Maym Kelso, Lucien Littlefield, Edna Mae Cooper, Jan Wolff.

With Bebe Daniels in Why Change Your Wife?

29. 1920: SOMETHING TO THINK ABOUT. Paramount. An
original Jeanie Macpherson scenario. Directed by Cecil
B. DeMille.

A blacksmith's daughter scorns a wealthy cripple's love
to marry a poor but rugged workman who is killed in a
subway accident. She returns home with her child to find
her father, blinded, hating her. She accepts the wealthy
cripple's offer of marriage, and learns to love him, al-
though he disdains her, until he too is regenerated.

CAST: Elliott Dexter, Theodore Roberts, Monte Blue,
Clair McDowell, Mickey Moore, Julia Faye.

With Elliott Dexter in Something to Think About.

30. 1920: THE GREAT MOMENT: Paramount. An original Elinor Glyn story. Directed by Sam Wood.

In her first starring vehicle at Paramount Swanson was a strong-willed English girl of noble family who falls in love with a virile American engineer, much to her father's disappointment. On a visit out West she is bitten on the breast by a rattlesnake, and the engineer-hero sucks out the venom and saves her life. The girl, unwilling to admit her true love and devotion, becomes a heartbreaker, and the hero grows ever stronger, sterner, and more silent. Eventually the lovers are reunited without another rattlesnake's assistance.

CAST: Milton Sills, Alec B. Francis, F. R. Butler, Helen Dunbar, Julia Faye.

With Milton Sills in The Great Moment.

Gloria in the conservatory in The Great Moment.

With F. R. Butler and Milton Sills in The Great Moment.

31. 1921: **THE AFFAIRS OF ANATOL.** Paramount. Suggested by
Arthur Schnitzler's play and the paraphrase thereof by
Granville Barker, with screenplay by Jeanie Macpherson.
Directed by Cecil B. DeMille.

A philandering husband finds each of his affairs a disappointment and returns each time gratefully to his wife,
Swanson, who understands him and is willing to wait.

CAST: Wallace Reid, Elliott Dexter, Bebe Daniels, Agnes
Ayres, Monte Blue, Wanda Hawley, Theodore
Roberts, Julia Faye, Theodore Kosloff, Polly
Moran, Raymond Hatton.

132

The Affairs of Anatol. *Top: Elliott Dexter, Wanda Hawley, and Wallace Reid. Bottom: Wallace Reid.*

Gloria looking vampirish in The Affairs of Anatol.

32. 1921: UNDER THE LASH. Paramount. Based on a novel, *The Shulamite,* by Claude & Alice Askew and a play by Askew & Ward Knoblock. Directed by Sam Wood.

A departure from glamor for Swanson, who played a drab, obedient, second wife of a stern Boerish farmer who rules by the lash. An Englishman comes to their African farm and opens a new vista to the wife by revealing to her the world of literature. But her husband misinterprets and is set to kill her, but the Englishman intervenes and saves her.

CAST: Mahlon Hamilton, Russell Simpson, Lillian Leighton, Lincoln Stedman.

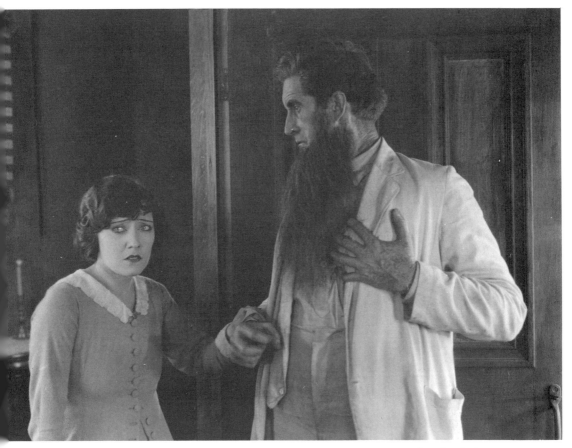

With Russell Simpson in Under the Lash.

With Russell Simpson and Mahlon Hamilton, Under the Lash.

In Under the Lash.

33. 1921: DON'T TELL EVERYTHING. Paramount. Directed by
Sam Wood.
Made largely of footage from an extra "affair" from the
Anatol film about a husband's escapade with an athletic
love, and expanded into a feature-length film.
CAST: Wallace Reid, Elliott Dexter, Dorothy Cumming.

Don't Tell Everything. *With Wallace Reid . . .*

. . . Elliott Dexter, Reid, and Dorothy Cummings . . .

. . . Cummings and Dexter . . .

with Reid and Cummings . . .

Reid, Cummings, and Dexter.

34. 1922. HER HUSBAND'S TRADEMARK. Paramount. Directed by Sam Wood.

An unscrupulous business man who uses his beautiful wife as a decoy in business schemes, throws her into the society of an old lover whom the husband wants to exploit in the promotion of his Mexican oil fields. The two fall in love, and the husband is killed by a Mexican bandit.

CAST: Richard Wayne, Stuart Holmes, Lucien Littlefield, Charles Ogle, Edythe Chapman, Clarence Burton, James Neill.

With Richard Wayne in Her Husband's Trademark.

With Stuart Holmes and Richard Wayne in Her Husband's Trademark.

35. 1922: BEYOND THE ROCKS. Paramount. Directed by Sam Wood.

Elinor Glyn wrote this pastiche specifically for Swanson and Valentino, but they did more for her than she for them. A poor aristocratic English girl just married to an elderly millionaire falls in love on her honeymoon with a young and handsome nobleman. This film was spliced with a number of period flashbacks so the lovers could be seen in the styles and manners of more romantic eras.

CAST: Rudolph Valentino, Edythe Chapman, Alec B. Francis, Gertrude Astor, Mabel Van Buren, Helen Dunbar, June Elvidge.

Beyond the Rocks *starred Gloria with Rudolph Valentino.*

Alec B. Francis was also featured in Beyond the Rocks.

Four romantic scenes featuring Gloria and Valentino.

A sickbed scene from Beyond the Rocks. *Valentino is on the left.*

Two women meet in Beyond the Rocks.

Eighteenth-century scenes from Beyond the Rocks.

The masked man is Valentino.

36. 1922: HER GILDED CAGE. Paramount. Based on an Ann
Nichols' play, *Love Dreams,* about the romance of Man-
uel of Portugal and Gaby Deslys, with scenario by Elmer
Harris. Directed by Sam Wood.

A French actress, hampered by an invalid sister and im-
poverished uncle, allows herself to be brought to America
billed as "Fleur d' amour," with publicity to link her
name with a king. Then she falls in love with an American artist.

CAST: David Powell, Harrison Ford, Anne Cornwall,
Walter Hiers, Charles A. Stevenson.

Gloria sports gay costumes in these two scenes from Her Gilded Cage.

From Her Gilded Cage.

37. 1922: **THE IMPOSSIBLE MRS. BELLEW.** Paramount. Directed
by Sam Wood.
A much-abused wife, struggling to keep her small son
from learning of his wasted father's scandalous conduct,
keeps silent in the divorce court, and so loses her good
name. She becomes the darling of Deauville, and eventually meets a real love who believes her.
CAST: Conrad Nagel, Frank Elliott, Robert Cain, Richard Wayne, June Elvidge, Herbert Standing,
Mickey Moore, Pat Moore, Helen Dunbar.

Gloria dressed as a mermaid in The Impossible Mrs. Bellew.

With director Sam Wood and Conrad Nagel on **The Impossible Mrs. Bellew** *set.*

38. 1923: MY AMERICAN WIFE. Paramount. Directed by Sam
    Wood.
    A dashing Spanish-American falls in love with a rich
    American girl, and is hounded and nearly killed by an
    Argentine villain. All ends well.
    CAST: Antonio Moreno, Josef Swickard, Gino Corrado,
    Eric Mayne, Edythe Chapman, Aileen Pringle,
    Walter Long, F. R. Butler, Loyal Underwood.

Gloria Swanson
in
"MY AMERICAN WIFE"
A Paramount Picture.

My American Wife: *Top, with Walter Long. Bottom, with Antonio Moreno.*

My American Wife. Edythe Chapman is at the far right.

39. 1923: PRODIGAL DAUGHTERS. Paramount. Directed by
    Sam Wood.
    A jazz-age daughter, fed up with the dictates of an old-
    fashioned father, leaves the family's Fifth Avenue man-
    sion, whoops it up in Greenwich Village, and returns
    home penitent in a heavy snowstorm on Christmas Eve.
    CAST: Ralph Graves, Vera Reynolds, Theodore Roberts,
           Louise Dresser, Charles Clary, Robert Agnew,
           Maude Wayne, Eric Mayne.

Gloria was featured with Theodore Roberts and Louise Dresser in these scenes from Prodigal Daughters.

40. 1923: BLUEBEARD'S EIGHTH WIFE. Paramount. Directed
by Sam Wood.

From an Alfred Savoir comedy in which Ina Claire starred
on Broadway, about a French girl who learns on the eve
of her marriage that her husband-to-be is popularly known
as "Bluebeard" because he has shed seven wives. Eight is
a lucky number for her, however, and she remains the
only woman in his life.

CAST: Huntley Gordon, Charles Greene, Robert Agnew,
        Paul Weigel, Lianne Salvor, F. R. Butler, Irene
        Dalton.

Gloria looks frightened in this scene from Bluebeard's Eighth Wife.

With Huntley Gordon in Bluebeard's Eighth Wi[

In Bluebeard's Eighth Wife.

41. 1923: **ZAZA.** Paramount. From the play by Pierre Barton &
Charles Simon. Directed by Allan Dwan.

Swanson was the devil-may-care Parisian soubrette who
falls in love with a married man, renounces him when
she learns he has a wife and child. Years later wife dies
and Zaza gets the true love she has waited for.

CAST: H. B. Warner, Ferdinand Gottschalk, Lucille La
Verne, Mary Thurman, Riley Hatch, Helen
Mack.

Gloria looking wistful in Zaza.

42. 1924: THE HUMMING BIRD. Paramount. Directed by Sidney
Olcott.

Based upon Maud Fulton's play about a Parisian gamine-
Apache who falls in love with a newspaper man in Paris
before World War I. When he goes to the front she re-
cruits the wolves of Montmartre and, disguised as one of
them, joins her husband at the front.

CAST: Edmund Burns, William Ricciardi, Cesare Gra-
vina, Mario Majeroni, Adrienne d'Ambricourt,
Helen Lindroth.

Two scenes from Hummingbird.

43. 1924: A SOCIETY SCANDAL. Paramount. Directed by Allan Dwan.

Based on Alfred Sutro's play, *The Laughing Lady*. A society wife deliberately ignores her husband's many indiscretions but when a caddish suitor forces his way into her bedroom her husband's mother so informs her son. There is a scandalous divorce, and the wife frames the attorney who has ripped her reputation to shreds. But she then decides she loves the attorney.

CAST: Rod La Rocque, Ricardo Cortez, Allan Simpson, Mrs. Ida Waterman.

With Rod LaRocque in A Society Scandal.

With Ricardo Cortez in A Society Scandal.

44. 1924: MANHANDLED. Paramount. Directed by Allan Dwan.
From an Arthur Stringer S.E.P. Cinderella story about a
department store salesgirl in love with a humble inventor.
She plays with fire in the bohemian set, is done over much
in the Pygmalion-Galatea way, finds high society not for
her, and is only too happy to be reinstated in the affections
of her inventor-lover who, without her knowing it, has
become a millionaire.

CAST: Tom Moore, Lilyan Tashman, Frank Morgan, Ian
Keith, Paul McAllister, Ann Pennington.

The advertisement for Manhandled.

Ian Keith and Gloria Swanson in Manhandled.

With Tom Moore in Manhandled.

Crowd scene in Manhandled.

On the subway (Manhandled).

45. 1924: HER LOVE STORY. Paramount. Directed by Allan Dwan.

From a Mary Roberts Rinehart tale about a Balkan queen who marries by gypsy ceremony the guardsman she really loves, and is then forced to marry the king of a neighboring country. When she bears a son and declares the baby's father to be the guardsman's, she is confined to a convent as insane. But she and her child are rescued by the guardsman.

CAST: Ian Keith, George Fawcett, Mario Majeroni.

With Ian Keith in Her Love Story.

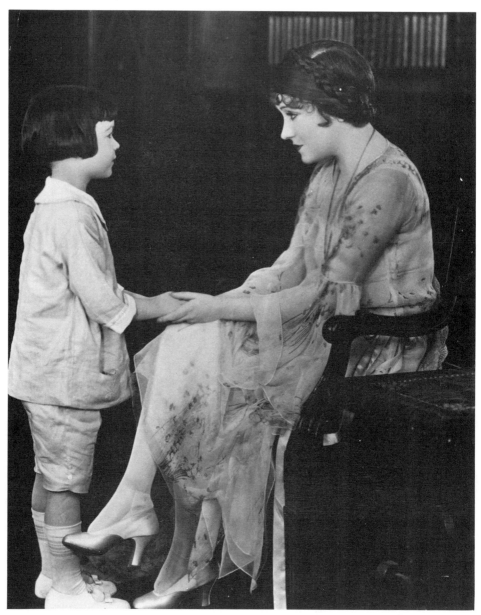

With young friend in Her Love Story.

Publicity shot for **Her Love Story.**

46. 1924: WAGES OF VIRTUE. Paramount. Directed by Allan
    Dwan.
    A Percival Wren Story, with Swanson as the darling of
    the French Foreign Legion in love with a young American
    soldier of fortune.
    CAST: Ben Lyon, Norman Trevor, Ivan Linow, Armand
       Cortez, Adrienne d'Ambricourt, Paul Panzer, Joe
       Moore.

Gloria mixes it up with male companions in The Wages of Virtue.

Gloria befriends soldier in The Wages of Virtue.

47. 1925: MADAME SANS-GENE. Paramount. Directed by Leonce
Perret. From the play by Victorien Sardou & Emile Mor-
eau.
The story of the French laundress who once did Napoleon's
laundry, becomes the wife of a Marshal, and isn't afraid
to tell the Emperor exactly what she thinks of him, because he still owes her for his laundry.
CAST: Charles de Roche, Warwick Ward, Emile Drain,
Arlette Marchal, Madeline Guitty.

Gloria starred with Charles de Roche, Warwick Ward, and Emile Drain in Madame Sans-Gene.

Outdoor scene in Madame Sans-Gene.

Gloria sports colorful outfit in Madame Sans-Gene.

48. 1925: THE COAST OF FOLLY. Paramount. Directed by Allan Dwan.

Swanson played a dual role—mother and daughter. A mother runs away from her only child and years later, when she is a tired titled plaything on the Riviera, finds her daughter is about to make the same mistake.

CAST: Alec B. Francis, Anthony Jowitt, Dorothy Cummings, Jed Prouty, Eugenie Besserer.

Advertisement for The Coast of Folly.

As the Countess de Tauro in The Coast of Folly.

49. 1925: STAGE STRUCK. Paramount. Directed by Allan Dwan. A comedy from a Frank R. Adams story about a waitress in a beanery with stage ambitions who ends up on an Ohio showboat, the *Water Queen.* It had a color sequence with Swanson as Salome, and a very amusing scene in which the fleas in a flea circus get loose and find themselves comfortable births on Swanson.

CAST: Lawrence Gray, Gertrude Astor, Marguerite Evans, Ford Sterling.

Gloria's dream of Salome in Stage Struck.

Gloria as a waitress in Stage Struck.

50. 1926: UNTAMED LADY. Paramount. Directed by Frank
     Tuttle.
     A Fannie Hurst story with Swanson as a spoiled daughter
     of the rich tamed by a strong-willed young man who
     happens to love her.
     CAST: Lawrence Gray, Joseph Smiley, Charles Graham.

With Lawrence Gray in Untamed Lady.

A scene from Untamed Lady.

51. 1926: FINE MANNERS. Paramount. Directed by Richard Rosson.
   Swanson played Orchid Murphy, a poor girl working in a burlesque theatre, courted by a millionaire who has his dowager aunt turn her into a fine lady, only to find he liked her better without the fine manners.
   CAST: Eugene O'Brien, Helen Dunbar, Walter Goss, John Miltern.

With Walter Goss in Fine Manners.

In Fine Manners.

52. 1927: THE LOVE OF SUNYA. United Artists. Directed by
Albert Parker. From the Max Marcin & Charles Guernon
play, *Eyes of Youth.*
Swanson played several variations of the same character.
As a young girl, at the turn of the road in her life, she is
able to see, when she looks into a crystal ball, each of the
road's turnings, and so settle for love rather than ambition
or wealth.
CAST: John Boles, Flobelle Fairbanks, Anders Randolph,
Adres De Segurola, Ian Keith, Hugh Miller, Ray-
mond Hackett, Pauline Garon, Ivan Lebedeff,
John Miltern.

With John Boles in The Love of Sunya.

With Raymond Hackett in The Love of Sunya.

In The Love of Sunya.

53. 1928: SADIE THOMPSON. United Artists. Directed by Raoul
Walsh. From the story by W. Somerset Maugham.

The story of a shady lady in Pago-Pago who didn't want to
go back to San Francisco because the police were waiting
for her and her clash with The Rev. Davidson, who trying
to save her soul, fell prey to her body and then killed himself. Swanson won an Academy Award nomination for
her performance.

CAST: Lionel Barrymore, Raoul Walsh, Blanche Frederici, Charles Lane, Florence Midgley, James A.
Marcus.

191

With Lionel Barrymore in Sadie Thompson.

Having a good time in Sadie Thompson.

In Sadie Thompson.

Advertisement for Sadie Thompson.

Publicity shot for Sadie Thomp

In Sadie Thompson.

With Raoul Walsh in Sadie Thompson.

54.   1928: QUEEN KELLY. Left unfinished; later reedited, new
        scenes shot and released on a limited basis. Directed by
        Erich von Stroheim from his own original screenplay. A
        mad queen of a mythical kingdom is betrothed to the
        handsome Prince Wolfram, but he falls in love with a
        convent girl, Kitty Kelly. He kidnaps her, and the queen,
        finding her, whips her unmercifully. The girl drowns her-
        self and is followed in death by the prince. A version put
        together by Swanson and shown in Europe and South
        America in the 30s, contains only a third of the projected
        story, with nothing of Swanson as Queen Kelly, owner
        of a string of South African brothels.
        CAST: Walter Byron, Seena Owen, Sidney Bracy, Tully
            Marshall (in excised African sequences).

Gloria Poses in a costume she wore in Queen Kelly.

With Seena Owen in Queen Kelly.

55. 1929: THE TRESPASSER. United Artists. Directed by Edmund Goulding.

Swanson's first talkie written by Goulding. She played a stenographer who marries a rich man's son, and when the marriage is annulled, fights to keep the son she has borne, accepting favors from her employer, so her child and she can exist in style. She won her second Academy Award nomination, and revealed a singing voice with the theme song, *Love Your Magic Spell Is Everywhere.*

CAST: Robert Ames, Henry B. Walthall, William Holden, Purnell Pratt, Wally Albright, Kay Hammond, Blanche Frederici, Mary Forbes, Marcelle Corday.

The Trespasser *was Gloria's first talkie.*

56. 1930: WHAT A WIDOW! United Artists, Directed by Allan Dwan.

A madcap farce with Swanson as a wealthy widow who sails for France, cuts up in Paris, and finally acquires an attractive husband. She sang several Vincent Youman songs.

CAST: Owen Moore, Lew Cody, Margaret Livingston, William Holden, Herbert Braggiotti, Gregory Gaye, Adrienne d'Ambricourt, Nella Walker, Daphne Pollard.

203

With Lew Cody (directly to Gloria's left) in What a Widow.

With Lew Cody in What a Widow.

In What a Widow.

With Owen Moore (in the middle on the left) in What a Widow.

57. 1931: INDISCREET. United Artists, Directed by Leo McCarey. Story & Songs by DeSylva, Brown & Henderson.

Swanson falls in love with an author who has written a book by which he tries to live, called *Obey that Impulse.* She tries to show her sister the rogue her sister's lover is, gets into other farcial situations, and ends up with the author, who decides he should have obeyed that impulse himself and gone after her sooner.

CAST: Ben Lyon, Arthur Lake, Monroe Owsley, Barbara Kent, Maude Eburne, Henry Kolker, Nella Walker.

In Indiscreet.

With Maude Eburne in Indiscreet. *(Gloria is singing "Come to Me.")*

With Monroe Owsley and Ben Lyon in Indiscreet.

With Barbara Kent and Arthur Lake in Indiscreet.

58. 1931: TONIGHT OR NEVER. United Artists. Directed by
Mervyn LeRoy. From David Belasco's last-produced play
by Lily Hatvany, screenplay by Ernest Vajda.
Swanson was a young prima donna affianced to a middle-
aged nobleman but in love with a mysterious and in-
triguing young man who turns out to be an operatic
impresario out to win her signature to a contract.
CAST: Melvyn Douglas, Ferdinand Gottschalk, Alison
Skipworth, Robert Greig, Warburton Gamble,
Greta Mayer, Boris Karloff.

Gloria and Gottschalk in three different moods in Tonight or Never.

Gloria in Tonight or Never.

59. 1933: A PERFECT UNDERSTANDING. United Artists. Directed by Cyril Gardner.

Filmed in England and the French Riviera, Swanson and Olivier were lovers who marry and then constantly misunderstand each other—but all is settled in the divorce courts and they go back together again as a man and wife who understand each other.

CAST: Laurence Olivier, John Halliday, Nigel Playfair, Michael Farmer, Genevieve Tobin, Nora Swinburne.

Gloria sports stylish outfit for A Perfect Understanding.

With John Halliday in A Perfect Understanding.

Scene from A Perfect Understanding. *Seated: Genevieve Tobin, Lawrence Olivier, Gloria, and (her real husband) Michael Farmer.*

With Genevieve Tobin in A Perfect Understanding.

With Lawrence Olivier in A Perfect Understanding.

60. 1934: MUSIC IN THE AIR. Fox. Directed by Joe May. From
the Kern-Hammerstein operetta.

Swanson is a temperamental diva who alternately fights
and romances her lyricist. When two naive peasants come
down from the Bavarian Alps to conquer Munich with
song, the quarrels become rectangular, until everybody
gets paired off happily.

CAST: John Boles, June Lang, Douglass Montgomery,
Al Shean, Reginald Owen, Joseph Cawthorn, Sara
Haden, Hobart Bosworth, Jed Prouty, Roger Im-
hoff, George Chandler, Marjorie Main, Ferdinand
Munier, Otis Harlan, Christian Rub, Fuzzy Knight.

With John Boles in Music in the Air.

With Douglass Montgomery and John Boles in Music in the Air.

With Douglass Montgomery in Music in the Air.

With Douglass Montgomery in Music in the Air.

61. 1941: FATHER TAKES A WIFE. RKO. Directed by Jack
Hively.
A shipping magnate weds a stage star and they start bick-
ering on their honeymoon. Their marital problems are
eventually solved by a stowaway Latin American singer.
CAST: Adolph Menjou, John Howard, Florence Rice,
Desi Arnaz, Neil Hamilton, Helen Broderick,
Grady Sutton, Mary Treen.

Advertisement for Father Takes a Wife, *Gloria's first picture in seven years.*

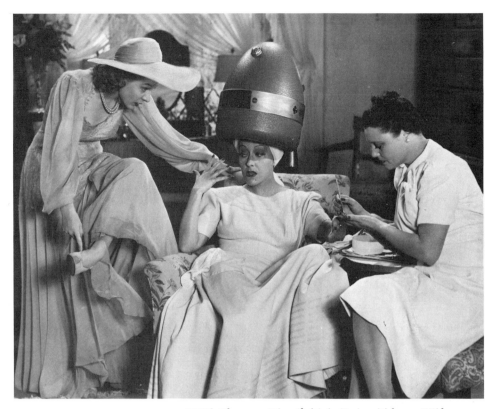

With Florence Rice (left) in Father Takes a Wife.

With Adolph Menjou in Father Takes a Wife.

62. 1949: DOWN MEMORY LANE. Eagle Lion. Directed by Phil Carlson. Film Clips of Sennett-produced silent and early talkies with all the players from the Keystone and later Sennett era, including several amusing Keystone bits showing the talents of young comedienne Swanson.

63. 1950: SUNSET BOULEVARD. Paramount. Directed by Billy Wilder.

Swanson as the ex-movie queen, Norma Desmond, who kills her young lover and returns to her glory days in a limbo of madness. She won her third Academy Award Nomination for this performance.

CAST: William Holden, Erich von Stroheim, Nancy Olsen, Cecil B. DeMille, Hedda Hopper, Fred Clark, Lloyd Gough, Jack Webb, Buster Keaton, Anna Q. Nilsson, H. B. Warner, Franklyn Farnum.

Three publicity poses.

Advertisement for Sunset Boulevard. *These, and the pictures that follow, record Gloria's remarkable comeback.*

Publicity shot with William Holden, Swanson, Nancy Olson and Erich Von Stroheim.

Gloria does Chaplin imitation, in this rare photographic sequence.

"It is to be a very important picture—the story of Salome."

Holden: "They've just repossessed my car."
Swanson: "Is that all? Have you ever seen an Isotta Fraschini?"

"Sometimes she'd have a bridge game with the waxworks."

"Sometimes she'd put on a show just for me. She'd call it, 'The Norma Desmond Follies.'"

"Do you want to see some more? Close your eyes—I'll be right back."

"Max, you're to get out the script and deliver it to Mr. DeMille in person."

"The point is, I've never looked better in all my life—because I've never been so happy in all my life."

Von Stroheim: "If madame will pardon me, the shadow over the left eye is not quite balanced."

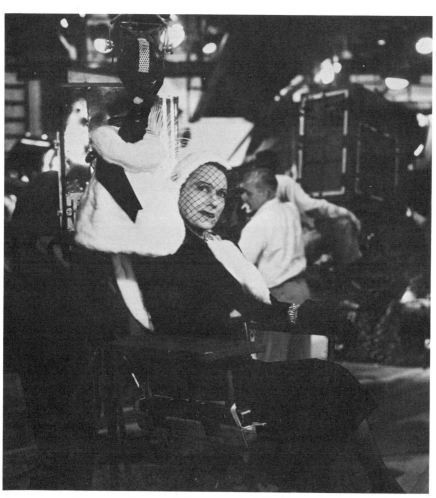

Swanson pushes away the microphone, symbolizing her rejection of the sound era.

"And remember darling, I don't work before ten in the morning, and never after 4:30 in the afternoon." (Cecil B. DeMille played himself in the film.)

"Those idiots, don't they know what a star looks like! I'll be up there again; I'll show them, so help me!"

"There are no other guests. We don't want to spoil the evening with others."

"Valentino said there's nothing like tile for the tango." (Note the famous painting of Gloria in the background. She loaned it for the making of the film.)

"*I'm rich. Own three blocks downtown. Got oil in Bakersfield—pumping, pumping, pumping.*"

"What you're trying to say is you don't want me to love you."

"Why don't you just say, 'thank you' and go."

"What is it you want; I'll give you anything you want. Is it money?"

"I suppose you think I made that up about the gun."

"DeMille only wanted to rent your car. No one has had the heart to tell you."

"The cameras have arrived? Tell Mr. DeMille I'll be on the set at once."

"You gentlemen must excuse me. I must get ready for my scene."

"I can't go on with the scene, I'm too happy. Mr. DeMille, do you mind if I say a few words? Thank you."

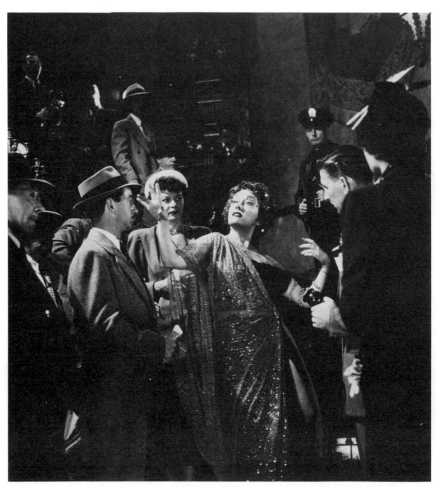

"I just want to tell you how happy I am, to be back in the studio, making a picture again."

"*I promise you I'll never desert you again. Because after* Salome *we'll make another picture.*"

"You see, this is my life. There's nothing else, just us, and the camera, and those wonderful people out there in the dark."

"All right, Mr. DeMille, I'm ready for my closeup."

64. 1952. THREE FOR BEDROOM C. Warner Bros. Directed by
    Milton H. Bren.
    A farce in Natural Color about a movie queen rushing
    back to Hollywood with fire in her eyes to protest against
    her new assignment. With no train reservation, she and
    her young daughter take over Bedroom C. and find it is
    that of a shy biochemistry professor on his way to Cal-Tech
    to give a lecture.
    CAST: James Warren, Fred Clark, Hans Conried, Steve
          Brodie, Janine Perreau, Ernest Anderson, Mar-
          garet Dumont.

With James Warren in Three for Bedroom C.

In Three for Bedroom C.

65. 1960: WHEN COMEDY WAS KING. 20th Century-Fox. Directed by Robert Youngson.
More clips from the early Sennett comedies, and others, many showing Swanson in her salad days as a slapstick comedienne.

Nero's Mistress, *Gloria's last film—to date.*

In Nero's Mistress.

66. 1962: NERO'S MISTRESS. Titanus-Manhattan. Directed by
Steno. An Eastman color satire on the private life of
Emperor Nero, who was terrified of his mother Agrippina,
played by Swanson. Filmed in 1956 but not released here
for six years.
CAST: Brigitte Bardot, Alberto Sordi, Vittorio De Sica,
Georgia Moll.

259

5

In Recent Years

In recent years, Gloria Swanson has become a familiar figure on television. She has appeared in various film series, proving that she has not lost her skill as an actress; and she has also made the rounds of television talk shows, where, in addition to discussing her career, she advocates the use of natural food products.

A longtime foe of food additives, Miss Swanson has recently been praised by one congressman for her role in getting cyclamates banned from grocery shelves.

Gloria meets John and Tim Considine on the set of a Straightaway *episode, 1961.*

("The Good Luck Charm," 1963).

("The Good Luck Charm," 1963).

With Gene Barry in a Burke's Law *episode, "Who Killed Vaudeville?" (1964).*

On the Mike Douglas talk show in 1964.

With Art Linkletter on Hollywood Talent Scouts, *1966.*

With Buddy Ebsen for a Beverly Hillbillies *episode, 1966.*

It was not until 1967 that Gloria Swanson made her Los Angeles stage debut in Reprise. *Lon Gardner is the actor pretending to be in a Zen trance.*